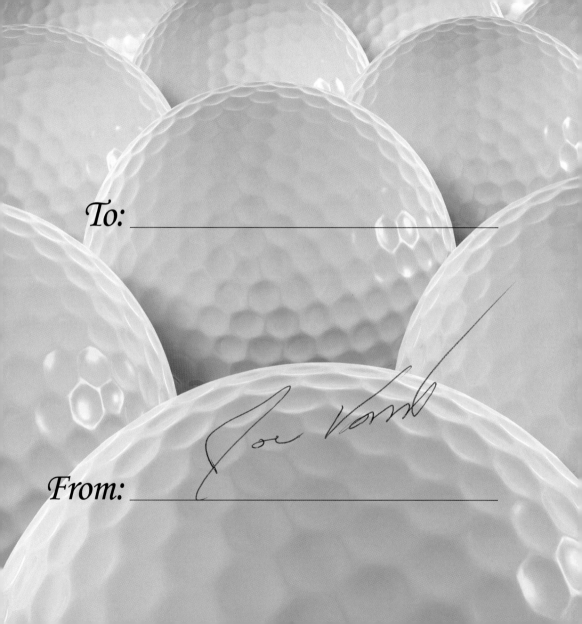

To: _____

From: _____

Design: Brian Frantz

Simple Truths is a registered trademark.
Printed and bound in the United States of America

ISBN 978-1-60810-109-2

800-900-3427
www.simpletruths.com

01 4CPG-LT 10

Photo Credits :

Cover : Durrance

Shutterstock : Dedication page, 4, 6, 18, 30, 36, 40, 42, 67

Dick Durrance II (durrance2@drinkerdurrance.com : 16, 22, 24, 28, 34, 70, 76, 124, 136, 154

Evan Schiller (golfshots@earthlink.net): 12, 46, 48, 52, 55, 58, 64, 72, 78, 82, 84, 88, 94, 97,
100, 106, 108, 112, 114, 118, 121, 130, 142, 144, 148, 151

Joann Dost (info@joanndost.com): 60, 90, 127, 133, 139

Istock : 10, 102

GOLF QUOTES

Great Quotes About a Great Game

Compiled by *Joe Vanek*

Introduction

Last spring, I played a round of golf at Arizona National with a friend, Steve, in Tucson. It was a beautiful day and the course was in perfect shape. Despite the conditions, the round started off a little rough for me – and for my friend as well. Steve's frustration was rising as the round progressed. His swing was a little off, and putts were just not dropping.

That's golf, so I offered a few words of encouragement – something about each hole being a new opportunity – and we played on. Neither of us knew then how true those words would become.

At the fifth hole, which is a par 5 that was playing about 510 yards, Steve hit a good – not great – drive just off the right side of the fairway, but it was long and left him 220 yards to the pin. Steve's second shot was a beauty. It landed just short of the pin, and with a couple of bounces and a short roll, left a 17 foot putt back to the hole. Frustration had turned to opportunity! And, when the putt went in for Steve's first eagle of his 40 plus year golfing life, it was the fulfillment of a journey. For that moment Steve could hang with the greats. The rest of the round was a footnote.

We both learned something that day that extended beyond a round of golf. Golf just tends to do that. The game is as perfect a window into the constitution of a man and the challenges of life as one can find. It is like a four hour interview, and it is a game played as much against one's self, as it is played against others. Perhaps that is why so much has been written about a game, and so many people have embraced a game that had modest origins in Scotland.

The strong link between golf and life is captured in the quotes compiled in this book. One of my favorites is by Gardner Dickinson, a professional golfer who competed from 1956 to 1971, and said: "They say golf is like life, but don't believe them. Golf is more complicated than that." Truer words could not have been spoken. So, sit back and enjoy the wisdom and wit that follows about the world's greatest game.

All the Best,

Joe Vanek

What other people may find in poetry or art museums,
I find in the flight of a good drive.

❧

Arnold Palmer

You swing your best when you have the fewest things to think about.

❧

Bobby Jones

*I*f a lot of people gripped a knife and fork the way
they do a golf club,
they'd starve to death.

Sam Snead

*Golf is so popular
simply because
it is the best game
in the world
at which to be bad.*

∞

A.A. Milne

*T*here is no room in your mind for negative thoughts. The busier you keep yourself with the particulars of shot assessment and execution, the less chance your mind has to dwell on the emotional. This is sheer intensity.

Jack Nicklaus

Black Diamond Ranch Golf & Country Club #15, Lecanto, FL

Baseball players quit playing and they take up golf.

Basketball players quit, take up golf.

Football players quit, take up golf.

What are we supposed to take up when we quit?

✺

George Archer

I have a tip that can take five strokes off anyone's golf game: it's called an eraser.

Arnold Palmer

*I*f you drink, don't drive. Don't even putt.

Dean Martin

Arrowhead Golf Club #10, Littleton, CO

*D*uffers who consistently shank their balls
are urged to buy and study
Shanks - No Thanks by R.K. Hoffman,
or in extreme cases,
M.S. Howard's excellent *Tennis for Beginners*.

Henry Beard

$\mathcal{G}$olf is a game that is played on a five-inch course – the distance between your ears.

Bobby Jones

One minute you're bleeding.
The next minute you're hemorrhaging.
The next minute you're painting the Mona Lisa.

Mac O'Grady

Forget your opponents;
always play against par.

❧

Sam Snead

The Golf Club at Ravenna #16, Littleton, CO

If profanity had an influence

on the flight of the ball,

the game of golf would be played

far better than it is.

❧

Horace G. Hutchinson

River Valley Ranch Golf Club #2, Carbondale, CO

They say golf is like life,
but don't believe them.
Golf is more complicated than that.

Gardner Dickinson

If you break 100, watch your golf.
If you break 80, watch your business.

Joey Adams

Sandia Golf Club #14, Albuquerque, NM

*M*an blames fate
for other accidents
but feels personally responsible
for a hole-in-one.

Martha Beckman

Golf appeals to the idiot in us and the child. Just how childlike golf players become is proven by their frequent inability to count past five.

John Updike

*I*f your opponent is playing several shots in vain
attempts to extricate himself from a bunker,
do not stand near him and audibly count his strokes.
It would be justifiable homicide if he wound up his pitiable
exhibition by applying his niblick to your head.

Harry Vardon

They call it golf because
all of the other four-letter words were taken.

Raymond Floyd

Robert Trent Jones Golf Club #11, Gainesville, VA

The golf swing is like a suitcase into which we are trying to pack one too many things.

John Updike

35

If you're caught on a golf course during a storm and are afraid of lightning, hold up a 1-iron. Not even God can hit a 1-iron.

Lee Trevino

*G*olf is played by twenty million mature American men whose wives think they are out having fun.

Jim Bishop

I'm hitting the woods just great, but I'm having a terrible time getting out of them.

Harry Toscano

$\mathcal{O}$ne of the most fascinating
things about golf
is how it reflects the cycle of life.
No matter what you shoot –
the next day you have to go back
to the first tee
and begin all over again
and make yourself
into something.

Peter Jacobsen

Golf isn't like other sports where you can take a player out if he's having a bad day. You have to play the whole game.

Phil Blackmar

Banff Springs Golf Club #10 - Banff, Alberta, Canada

*I*nvariably something happens at a U.S. Open where the golf course gets out of control one day, they have one pin that's out of control. It always seems to happen. But they've gotten better about the height of the rough.

Payne Stewart

*T*revino is in a league by himself.
We don't even count him.
We figure when you come in second,
you're a winner.

∽

Chi Chi Rodriguez

Troon North Golf Club - Pinnacle Course #6 - Scottsdale, AZ

*R*everse every natural instinct and
do the opposite of what you are inclined to do,
and you will probably come very close
to having a perfect golf swing.

Ben Hogan

I'm a golfaholic, no question about that.

Counseling wouldn't help me.

They'd have to put me in prison,

and then I'd talk the warden into building

a hole or two and teach him how to play.

Lee Trevino

Big Sky Golf & Country Club #8 - Whistler, BC

Golf is a game in which the ball lies poorly
and the players well.

Art Rosenbaum

*G*olf is the most fun you can have without taking your clothes off.

Chi Chi Rodriguez

El Dorado Golf & Beach Club #10 - Los Cabos, Mexico

The only time my prayers
are never answered
is on the golf course.

Billy Graham

*I*sn't it fun to go out on the course
and lie in the sun?

Bob Hope

Old Head Golf Links #12 - Kinsale Co. Cork Republic of Ireland

If you wish to hide your character,
do not play golf.

Percey Boomer

*G*olf can best be defined
as an endless series
of tragedies obscured
by the occasional miracle.

Author Unknown

Challenge at Manele #12, Lana'i, HI

What's nice about our tour is you can't remember your bad shots.

Bob Bruce, about the senior tour

*I play in the low 80s.
If it's any hotter than that,
I won't play.*

Joe E. Lewis

Don't play too much golf. Two rounds a day are plenty.

Harry Vardon

St. Andrews Links - The Old Course #18, St. Andrews, Scotland

*F*ind a man with both feet
firmly on the ground
and you've found a man
about to make a difficult putt.

≈

Fletcher Knebel

Cornerstone Club #11, Montrose, CO

Do your best,

one shot at a time and then move on.

Remember that golf is just a game.

Nancy Lopez

xercise?
I get it on the golf course.
When I see my friends collapse,
I run for the paramedics.

Red Skelton

Bethpage State Park - Black Course #17 - Farmingdale, NY

Go out and have fun.
Golf is a game for everyone,
not just for the talented few.

∞

Harvey Penick

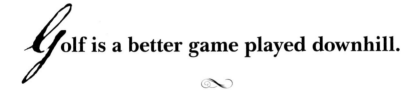

Golf is a better game played downhill.

Jack Nicklaus

The Links at Cougar Canyon Golf Club #16, Trinidad, CO

$\mathcal{G}$olf is a matter
of confidence.
If you think you
cannot do it,
there is no chance
you will.

❧

Henry Cotton

Golf is a puzzle without an answer. I've played the game for 40 years and I still haven't the slightest idea how to play.

Gary Player

The Creek Club at Reynolds Plantation #6, Greensboro, GA

*G*olf is deceptively simple and endlessly complicated. It satisfies the soul and frustrates the intellect. It is at the same time rewarding and maddening – it is without a doubt the greatest game mankind has ever invented.

∞

Arnold Palmer

Golf is not a game of good shots.
It's a game of bad shots.

Ben Hogan

Golf is the hardest game in the world.
There is no way you can ever get it.
Just when you think you do,
the game jumps up and puts you in your place.

Ben Crenshaw

Hualalai Golf Club - Nicklaus #17 - Kailua Kona, HI

I have come to understand and appreciate writers much more recently since I started working on a book last fall. Before that, I thought golf writers got up every morning, played a round of golf, had lunch, showed up for our last three holes and then went to dinner.

Phil Mickelson

Pinnacle Point #6 - Mossel Bay, South Africa

Golf ... is the infallible test.
The man who can go into
a patch of rough alone,
with the knowledge that
only God is watching him,
and play his ball where it lies,
is the man who will serve
you faithfully and well.

P. G. Wodehouse

I enjoy Augusta.
I enjoy its challenges.
There's no other golf course like this anywhere.

Its greens and its challenges on and around the greens

are just super, super tough. So the greens are fun to

play in sort of a morbid way.

Ben Crenshaw

Pezula Resort Hotel & Spa #14 - Knysna, South Africa

*G*olf without bunkers and hazards
would be tame and monotonous.
So would life.

B. C. Forbes

90

I'm not feeling very well –
I need a doctor immediately.
Ring the nearest golf course.

Groucho Marx

Experience at Koele #17, Lana'i, HI

I've really got no complaints about the way I played,

just extremely frustrating with the putter

and I'm sure there's a lot of other players

saying the same thing except the guy

who's going to win the golf tournament.

Greg Norman

If there's a golf course in heaven,

I hope it's like Augusta National.

I just don't want an early tee time.

Gary Player

Sun River Golf Course #9 - Sunriver, OR

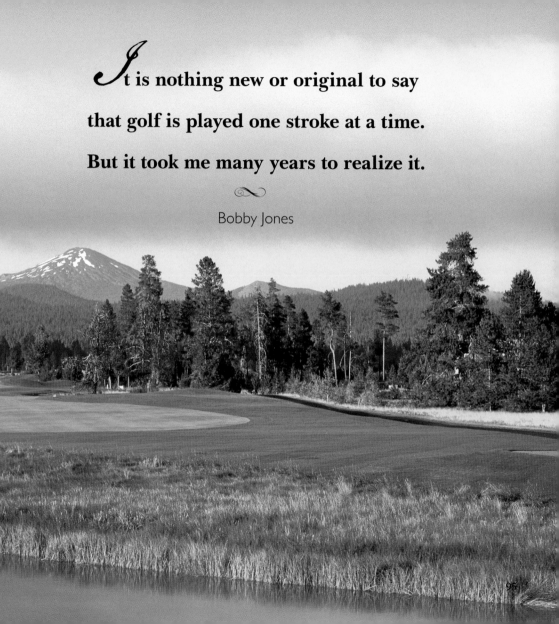

$\mathcal{I}$t is nothing new or original to say

that golf is played one stroke at a time.

But it took me many years to realize it.

Bobby Jones

*P*lacing the ball in the right position
for the next shot is eighty percent
of winning golf.

∾

Ben Hogan

The Golf Club at Terra Lago - North Course #6 - Palm Spring, CA

Kauai Lagoons Kiele Club - Kiele Course #13 - Kauai, HI

Success in golf depends less on strength of body than upon strength of mind and character.

Arnold Palmer

*T*hat's what makes the Ryder Cup in golf

so much better than the Masters or the U.S. Open.

To be a part of something that is not about personal

achievement, but about representing everyone and

sharing it with the whole country, it's wonderful.

Scott Hamilton

Indian Wells Golf Resort - Celebrity #16 - Palm Springs, CA

*T*here is no similarity between golf and putting; they are two different games, one played in the air, and the other on the ground.

❧

Ben Hogan

There is no such thing as natural touch.

Touch is something you create

by hitting millions of golf balls.

❧

Lee Trevino

Luana Hills Country Club #8 - Kailua, HI

*T*o be consistently effective,

you must put a certain distance

between yourself and what happens

to you on the golf course.

This is not indifference,

it's detachment.

Sam Snead

To play well you must feel tranquil and at peace.

I have never been troubled by nerves

in golf because I felt I had nothing to lose

and everything to gain.

Harry Vardon

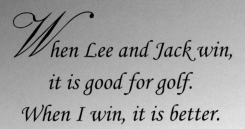

*When Lee and Jack win,
it is good for golf.
When I win, it is better.*

Chi Chi Rodriguez

112

Coyote Moon Golf Course #16 - Truckee, CA

Years ago we discovered the exact point,
the dead center of middle age.
It occurs when you are too young
to take up golf and too old
to rush up to the net.

Franklin Pierce Adams

Coyote Moon Golf Course #12 - Truckee, CA

Golf tips are like aspirin.
One may do you good,
but if you swallow the whole bottle,
you will be lucky to survive.

∽

Harvey Penick

Montammy Golf Club #16 - Alpine, NJ

*N*o man has mastered golf
until he realizes
that his good shots are accidents
and his bad shots are good exercise.

Eugene R. Black

Bear Mountain, Valley Course #3 - Victoria, BC

*G*olf is like fishing and hunting.
What counts is the companionship
and fellowship of friends,
not what you catch or shoot.

❧

George Archer

Ballyneal Golf & Hunt Club #6, Holyoke, CO

*A*ll seasoned players know,

or at least have felt,

that when you are playing your best,

you are much the same

as in a state of meditation.

You're free of tension and chatter.

You are concentrating on one thing.

It is the ideal condition for good golf.

❧

Harvey Penick

The Quarry at La Quinta #5, La Quinta, CA

I didn't miss the putt.

I made the putt.

The ball missed the hole.

Peter Jacobsen

I have always had a drive that pushed me to try for perfection, and golf is a game in which perfection stays just out of reach.

Betsy Rawls

Ventana Canyon Golf Club - Canyon Course #13, Tucson, AZ

I've always made a total effort,
even when the odds seemed entirely against me.
I never quit trying;
I never felt that I didn't have a chance to win.

Arnold Palmer

*Putts get real difficult
the day they hand out the money.*

∽

Lee Trevino

Quail Lodge Resort & Golf Club #17, Carmel Valley, CA

LPGA International Legends Course #11, Daytona Beach, FL

He's been a top player
for the last 10 years,
and we all work on our swings,
we all change things.
We keep working and then we're
trying to get better,
and sometimes you get worse
trying to get better.
You've just got to give it some
time, be patient for
it to turn around, and when it
does turn around,
you feel like you can start
winning again.

Ernie Els

When your shot has to carry
over a water hazard,
you can either hit one
more club or two more balls.

Henry Beard

St. Andrews Links - The Old Course #18, St. Andrews, Scotland

I would like to deny all allegations by Bob Hope that during my last game of golf, I hit an eagle, a birdie, an elk and a moose.

❧

Gerald Ford

It took me seventeen years to get

3,000 hits in baseball.

I did it in one afternoon on the golf course.

Hank Aaron

*T*here are two basic rules
which should never be broken.
Be subtle.
And don't, for God's sake,
try to do business with anyone
who's having a bad game.

William Davis

Bethpage State Park - Black Course #15 - Farmingdale, NY

*The only thing you should force
in a golf swing is the club back in the bag.*

Byron Nelson

Ko'olau Golf Club #15 - Oahu, HI

If you think your hands are more important
in your golf swing than your legs,
try walking a hole on your hands.

∞

Gary Player

Old Head Golf Links #7 - Kinsale Co. Cork Republic of Ireland

149

*F*orget the last shot.

It takes so long to accept

that you can't always replicate your swing.

The only thing you can control

is your attitude toward the next shot.

Mark McCumber

Bay Harbor Golf Club - The Quarry #9 - Bay Harbor, MI

*R*eal pressure in golf is playing
for $10 when you've only got $5 in your pocket.

Lee Trevino

No other game combines the wonder of nature with the discipline of sport in such carefully planned ways. A great golf course both frees and challenges a golfer's mind.

Tom Watson

he object of golf
is not just to win.
It is to play like a gentleman,
and win.

Phil Mickelson

La Paloma Country Club - Hill Course #6, Tuscon, AZ

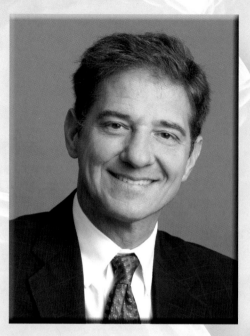

Joe Vanek is a husband, father, attorney and entrepreneur who lives in Clarendon Hills, Illinois. In addition to practicing law in the fields of antitrust, intellectual property and commercial litigation, Joe has successfully started a series of companies. Most recently, Joe co-founded an electronic voting machine company known as AutoMark that developed a device designed to assist individuals with disabilities gain full access to the voting process. Today, over fifty percent of the precincts in America use the AutoMark. Joe also assisted Mac Anderson when he created Simple Truths.

Joe is a member of Edgewood Valley Country Club located in Willow Springs, Illinois and may be contacted at jvanek@vaneklaw.com.

simple truths®
THE GIFT OF INSPIRATION

If you have enjoyed this book we invite you to check out our entire collection of gift books, with free inspirational movies, at **www.simpletruths.com.**

You'll discover it's a great way to inspire *friends* and *family,* or to thank your best *customers* and *employees.*

For more information, please visit us at:

www.simpletruths.com

Or call us toll free …

800-900-3427